Embracing the Heart of Christ

A JOURNEY OF GRIEF, HEALING, AND HOPE

Gerard P. Fleming

Father of Ambrose Augustine Fleming

Published by Mater Media
St. Louis, Missouri
www.matermedia.org

Cover and Interior Design: Trese Gloriod

ISBN: 979-8-9887392-8-9

Starting with Prayer

Dear Lord,

Help us heal. Whenever I hear about a parent suffering from the death of a child, I feel deep, compassionate sorrow. I also feel helpless and even at a loss for words. Dear Lord, I ask that you send all your angels and saints, including my son, into the hearts of these grieving parents. Let these parents know that you have conquered death and that their child is safe in your house, not dead and gone but alive and full of joy.

Amen

Introduction

I am sorry that you have experienced the death of someone so dear to you. You are not alone. The concept of us all being one body in Christ became better understood during and after the death of my son. When one of us suffers, we all suffer; when one of us rejoices, we all rejoice. By sharing our joys and sorrows, we learn our faith, how to love, and how to have hope. In that spirit, I share this journal prayer book with you. It's a collection of my reflections and prayers from the first few years after Ambrose's drowning. I pray that the time you invest in reading, reflecting, and praying with this devotional:

- expresses your heart, thoughts, feelings, and faith;
- brings comfort and heightens your hope;
- invokes a sense of gratitude for the gifts God has given;
- helps you feel Christ's endless love and mercy pour down upon you; and
- inspires you to invite Jesus into your heart, lift up your head, and pour His love upon others

The 12th Station: Jesus Dies on the Cross, statue at La Salle Retreat Center in Wildwood, Missouri.

Where was Jesus?

Theme: Finding Jesus in Our Suffering
Scripture: John 2:1-12

I avoid thinking about the tragic day Ambrose drowned. Months after Ambrose's death, my brother, Fr. Rodger Fleming asked me about that day. I told him I didn't want to think or talk about it. He wisely continued and asked me where I thought Jesus was that day. It felt like a question out of left field. I thought, "Where was Jesus!? I don't know. I didn't see him." Yet, I knew my brother was providing sound spiritual counsel, so I took his question seriously and tried to imagine where He might have been. But, still, I couldn't picture Jesus present.

Fast-forward two years to a gospel reading I read during a retreat. I reflected on the reading, attempting a Lectio Divina approach in which you look for a phrase that speaks to you, meditate on it, pray about it, and then sit quietly with it.

As I read John 2:1-12. I didn't make it past the first verse before I knew which phrase the Holy Spirit was guiding me to: "The mother of Jesus was there." It was like the phrase was in bold font and stood alone on the page. I read it repeatedly.

The following verse indicates that Jesus and the disciples were there, too. Mary was there, and she brought her son with her. And with him came the whole community of saints. They were all around us, covering us in true love and genuine compassion.

While paramedics were hopelessly performing CPR, and I fell to the ground in an agonizing scream, Jesus was in the garden of Gethsemane. Mary, my mother, was there too. She witnessed her Son being scourged and suffering, and her love and heartache fell upon us.

When my sweet wife, Susan, hugged and consoled others in anguish, Jesus consoled the women while he carried His heavy cross. Mary was beside Susan, helping her speak words of faith and trust in God, no matter the outcome.

When Susan bathed Ambrose's filthy body with the white hospital cloths, Veronica wiped Jesus' bloody face.

As we witnessed Ambrose's life pass away in the hospital, Mary stood at the foot of the cross right by our sides. She held us up as we leaned on one another.

When Susan held Ambrose's lifeless body, Mary held Jesus in that Pieta moment.

As Ambrose passed from this world to the next, he gave up his body, enabling others to live through the gift of organ donation. When Jesus gave up his body in what appeared to be a tragic moment, he conquered death and gave us life.

"Where was Jesus?" my brother asked. I was blind and didn't see Him, but Jesus has healed my blindness, and now I see.

Compassion means "to suffer together." That's where Jesus and Mary were. They were there with us, suffered with us, and showered us in love.

The mother of Jesus was there, and she brought her Son.

Questions for Reflection:

1. Where was Jesus on your tragic date?
2. Have you leaned on Mary in your sorrow?
3. How have others shared Christ's compassionate love with you?

An Empty Pair of Sandals

Hi Ambrose,

I read about Seder meal traditions, and the questions children ask about the lamb, matzo, moror, and haroses. The tradition keeps essential memories and lessons alive. In part, it helps us give thanks for Christ, who came down from heaven to be broken for us in this holy season.

I wonder what traditions we should establish to help us all remember you and live out the lessons you taught us.

I have the sandals you wore on that tragic day, and they are coming to the forefront of my mind as I reflect on this. You filled those sandals on the way to Grandma's home. Days later, I brought home those empty sandals and carried them into the house.

I cannot count how many times I carried your beautiful sleeping body into the house after a road trip. But this time, I was carrying an empty pair of sandals.

I recall struggling with what to do with those sandals. Where do I set them down? I didn't know.

I eventually carefully placed them in the basement shoe bin. They are there and available for Vianney to grow into.

But perhaps these are sandals that only you will have walked in. Maybe they are memorials of your joy and life. I don't know, though, because they will always remind me of the day I brought you to Grandma's, full of life and joy, and we returned home with an empty pair of sandals.

I guess that tragic day and the loss of you will always be a memory for me. Your sandals will remind me of how fragile and precious life is and to show love today while I have the opportunity. Let the sandals remind me how you and Christ gave up your bodies so others can live.

I love you, Ambrose. Help me to remember to love. Help me remember to sacrifice myself for the needs of others. Help me to be more like you, less of me, and more like Christ. Let your empty sandals remind me to lessen and Christ to increase.

Thank you, Ambrose. Thank you, Christ.
Love, Dad

Questions for Reflection:

1. Have you created any memorials?
2. What lessons has the death of your loved one taught you?
3. How do you honor your loved one's life? What legacy are you enabling them to leave?

A New Season

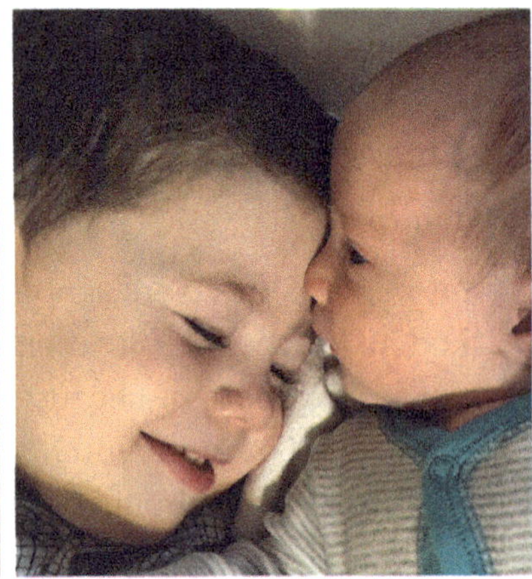

Good morning, Ambrose.

It is a beautiful morning. I looked out our front picture window as the morning sun shined through the clouds creating a beautiful hue. My view includes your memorial bench sitting on the front porch in front of my window with the two Ambrose memorial wind chimes hanging above it. The gentle breeze sounded soft melodic chimes. It's you. I told Jack, Blaise, and Isaac, that the wind chimes remind me you are here even though we cannot see you.

I hear the chimes playing in the background as I type this up and even see them in the reflection of my laptop as they sway before the sunshine and spring morning.

It has been 6 months and a new season has started. Vianney is sitting next to me, looking up to me, resting his head on me, smiling at me, babbling at me, and looking as cute as can be. He is a joy. He helps us see that life continues and will always have purpose and meaning.

Yet, as I look upon him, I am also saddened that he will not have you as his buddy brother growing up.

But then again, as the chimes dance in the wind, I am reminded you are still here, and you will be there for him at every moment.

Ambrose, thank you!

Love, Dad

Questions for Reflection:

1. As seasons have passed, how has your grief experience changed?
2. What seasonal events remind you of your loved one?
3. What reminds you that your child or loved one is not dead and gone but alive and full of joy?

Albert Gyorgy's sculpture entitled "Melancholy."
Photo by art_inthecity posted to Flickr. CC BY 2.0

Lord, Lift Up My Head

Theme: Loving Others Through Our Suffering
Scripture: John 5:1-9

Good morning, Ambrose, my sweet son.

I miss you desperately today. However, I have decided to lift my head, raise my spirits this morning, and recognize the gift of this day.

I have seen this statue posted several times with comments indicating that it reflects how it feels to lose a child. And it is 100% true. It captures the sorrow and emptiness I have felt.

But that is only part of the image. That is when I choose to sit alone on that bench. That is when I look down and focus on myself.

Today, I opened a prayer book that once belonged to my dad. The last line of the passage read, "Thou, O Lord, art my protector, my glory, and the lifter up of my head." That immediately brought this statue image to my mind.

Ambrose, with your help, I ask this of the Lord:

Lord, lift up my head. Help me see your goodness. Help me see my beautiful wife beside me, my children sitting with me, my friends supporting me, and others sitting on their own benches.

I choose you, O Lord. I choose to see you. I choose to fill my emptiness with your love. Transplant my broken, stony heart with your loving, sacred heart. I choose to get up off this bench and to love those you put around me.

Today, with the help of my sweet son and my dear Lord, may I lift up my head and see the glory of God.

Amen

Questions for Reflection:

1. Is the Lord calling me to pick up my mat and walk?
2. Who else is suffering? How can I be there for them?
3. Who am I grateful for? How can I share my gratitude?

Good Grief

This grief of mine! Sometimes, it's like I have put it away in a box and closed the lid. Yet, the container isn't airtight, and the pain is unconsciously ever-present.

At other times, the pressure seems to build up, and the cover bursts off, causing an eruption of sorrow and suffering. Then, there are times when I purposely choose to remove the lid and gently hold the grief in my hands. The outcome can be a good cry and a recollection of fond memories.

Today is different than any of those. It's more like the lid is wide open, but the sorrow remains within the box. It's contained, yet I'm fully aware of its presence.

I'm not sure if any of this makes sense. After last night's eruption, this "box" description of my grief experience came to mind. I figured I'd put it into words as I tried to make sense of it.

I realize this box is something I'll carry with me for the rest of my life. Perhaps I hold onto it because it is something I have of him. In a way, because I grieve, he is.

But the grief isn't an unhealthy illusion that he is physically present. And I try not to let my grief be a pile of regret. Instead, it is a longing to be with him once again. I remind myself that I will join him and not the other way around. He is already where I long to be. In this way of grieving, the box can be viewed as a hope chest, holding memories and love in anticipation of seeing him again.

And the hope is not only in seeing him, but also in seeing others for whom I grieve, particularly my parents. The hope goes far beyond seeing loved ones who have passed; it is also for those I live with and love today, especially my wife and children. One day, we will all die. My son is ahead of us on this journey, and he is where I long for all my loved ones to be. I have a part to play in ensuring we will be together for eternity. How I embark on this journey is crucial. I will seek God's grace so that I may grow in faith. I will allow Christ into my heart so that I can extend His love to others. I will heighten my hope and trust in God's salvation and eternal happiness with God and the community of saints, including my son.

I will carry this hope chest with me throughout the journey. And I vow it will be my fuel, propelling me to the destination rather than weighing me down. It will be good grief.

Questions for Reflection:

1. How would you describe your grief?
2. How do you manage your grief?
3. What purpose does your grief serve?

The image of Mary praying over Susan and Ambrose was created by Terrence St. Hilaire and commissioned as a gift to us.

Mary, My Mother

Today, I pulled up the "Mary My Mother" prayer and prayed it again for the first time in many months.

I first prayed it around July 2018 when Mom was approaching the end of her life. I was in our family room, alone and looking at the Divine Mercy Jesus image and the image of Mary hanging on our wall. I was angry with God. I asked him why he was taking my mother away from me and this world. I told God I needed my mother, and the world needed her. She was so close to Christ that others could know Christ by knowing her. Distraught, I dropped my head and closed my eyes. As I opened them again, a prayer card came into focus on the floor in front of me. It had a picture of Mary on one side and this prayer on the other:

Mary, my Mother,
I give my all to you;
to you I entrust all that I am;
All that I have and all that I do.
Help me to surrender ever
more fully to the Holy Spirit
so that the light of God may shine upon me
each day of my life.
Lead me deeper into the Mystery of the cross
and the fullness of faith
so that I may radiate Christ's endless love
and mercy to others.

Can you imagine what I felt after reading the very first line? It read, "Mary, my mother." I had just finished complaining to God that He was taking away my mother, and what did Mary, my mother, do? She reminded me that she was present, that she was my compassionate Mother, and that she would always be there for me.

During His suffering and death, Jesus gave me my mother for all time. Mary's gentle reminder also helped me realize that I was not losing Mom but that she was joining Mary and Christ, and she, too, would remain with me forever.

Mary challenged and encouraged me in this prayer. After reading it, I knew three things. 1) My mom was going to die soon, 2) Mary and my mom will always be there for me, 3) I could no longer bask in Mom's reflective glow but was being called to radiate Christ's love and mercy myself.

I could see this was not going to be easy for me. Look at the words! By praying this prayer, I was asking to better surrender to the Holy Spirit—not my will, but yours. Yikes! Then, in the last verse, "Lead me deeper into the Mystery of the cross." Double yikes!! This is one of those prayers you know is good for you, but you aren't sure you want to be answered.

Reviewing this prayer after Ambrose's passing, I see that God has been answering my prayers. I am still not sure I like it, but I learned to surrender, bringing me closer to Christ. My first journal prayer posted on the CaringBridge site was my surrender to God's will: "I guess I must let go and trust in you." I do not think I knew what surrender was until that moment. O Lord, thank you for teaching me despite the pain of the lesson.

And then, I was led more deeply into the Mystery of the cross. Oh, the suffering. Oh, the pain. Oh, the power of the love felt from others helping to carry the cross. The beauty of giving up one's life so others can live. The recognition of how much God the Father loves us—to have given us His only Son. The agony in a mother's face as she holds her lifeless son. And how much more spectacular is the resurrection! The joy of finding Christ alive again, and the hope of eternal life. How much more I appreciate being the recipient of the sacrificed and donated Body of Christ.

Mary, My Mother,

Thank you for putting this prayer before me, knowing what is best for me, and guiding me to Christ.

Mom, I feel your love. I know you are with me through all of this and that I will one day be with you again. Help me to radiate Christ's endless love and mercy to others like you.

Amen

Questions for Reflection:

1. Did you get angry with God?
2. Have you learned to surrender to God's will?
3. How has Mary, our mother, encouraged you?
4. Have you found that your suffering has deepened your understanding, wisdom, or faith?

Eight Minus One Is So Much Less Than Seven

Shortly after Ambrose's death, I recall sitting at our family dinner table, unsure whether everyone was present. It felt like a few kids were missing, so I counted them. Seven, everyone was there. Yet, it just seemed so much fewer than just one child missing from our family dinner table. It felt so much quieter, smaller, and less.

It is not that Ambrose was the loudest or biggest. Far from it. But his absence was as loud and big as the fireworks grand finale on the 4th of July.

I thought to myself, eight minus one is so much less than seven.

I have continued to feel his absence and know that I will miss him until I am blessed enough to see him again in heaven. Oh, what a joyous day that will be!

In the meantime, I have decided that eight is eight and always will be. When asked how many kids I have, the answer is eight. When the wind chimes dance and the cardinal lands on the fence nearby, Ambrose makes his presence known. When I count out my kids to ensure everyone is present, it goes like this, "Jack, Isaac, Blaise, Geena, Tobias, Agnes, Ambrose is in heaven, and Vianney. When he seems to be missing from his seat in the kayak, his absence is saying hello. When the kids pick up his toothbrush and ask what we shall do with this, he laughs because he does not have to brush his teeth. When I go to the park and see a young child dancing through the sprinklers with a giant grin, I see his smile. When I run into a little boy in the back of church wearing his same brown sandals, he reminds me to be more like him, less of me, and more like Christ.

He remains a part of our lives. He is not gone but only ahead of us on the journey. There is no "minus 1". There remain eight, and God willing, in January, there will be nine. God is good!

Questions for Reflection:

1. How have you felt the absence of your loved one?
2. How have you felt your loved one's presence?
3. How do you respond to the question of "How many children do you have?"

Blessed are they who dwell in your house!

Scripture: John 11:1-45

Dear Lord,

My soul yearns to dwell in your presence. My heart and my flesh cry out for the living God. Blessed are they who dwell in your house and continually praise you. Psalm 84

Lord, I most certainly wanted a Lazarus-like miracle for my son, Ambrose. When he was in the hospital and even after he was in the grave, I imagined him rising from his death and returning to me.

But, like Martha, I have come to believe that you are Christ, the Son of God. You are the resurrection and the life and Ambrose will never die. My son eternally dwells in your presence. I'd rather Ambrose dwell in the house of my God than return to a temporary worldly home.

How lovely is your dwelling place, my Lord, mighty God! My soul yearns to dwell in your presence. My heart and flesh cry out to you. Blessed are they who dwell in your house and continually praise you.

Amen

Questions for Reflection:

1. Is it selfish of us to wish for our loved ones to return to earth?
2. Jesus wasn't there to prevent Lazarus' death and indicates it was for "the greater glory of God". Is it possible, your loved one's death and non-resurrection, is for the greater glory of God?
3. Are you yearning to dwell in God's presence?

Trusting in Christ in the Calm and in the Storm

Scripture: Matthew 14:22-36

Dear Lord,

I'm reflecting on Matthew's writing about the storm and the boat. The first line of today's reading, "Jesus had the disciples get into a boat and proceed him to the other side." I'm still not sure if this has any significant meaning but it does show trust in you and following you regardless of the weather. That is, they didn't just call on you in the storm, but they followed your word in the calm. There's also something about you telling them to get into the boat when you knew a storm was coming. You knew! Of course, you knew. Yet you also knew they would be safe. You knew there would be growth in faith among the disciples from the experience. You knew that the experience would increase their trust in you. You knew that they would share this story and help others grow in faith and trust in you. You knew that I would read this story and it would help me trust in you.

During the storm of Ambrose's dying, thanks to the prayers of others, you held me up from sinking into a sea of despair. The winds were strong and scary, yet there I stood. Not only was I able to stand but I was able to show my kids that while this was horrific, we were safe in your presence. Yes, I was scared and yes, I began to sink but I called on you and you answered. My kids sat in the boat and watched and learned to trust in you. For that, I am forever grateful.

Dear Jesus, truly you are the Son of God. Help me to trust in you and follow you in the calm and through the storms, all the days of my life. Thank you to all those who have prayed for us and helped us through this storm.

I love you and trust in you. Help me to love you and trust in you more.

Amen

Questions for Reflection:

1. What does Christ sending his disciples out into the storm say to you about His divine providence?
2. How can Jesus' presence in the midst of the storm inspire you to find hope and courage in your own turbulent times?
3. Has God used your storm to deepen your faith and trust in God's divine plan?
4. Have you, like Peter, called out to Jesus to save you?

Everything Belongs to God

This weekend, at the Catholic Family Conference, Susan and I heard Kimberly Hahn say, "Everything belongs to God. Everything. Our works, our possessions, and even our children." I was walking with Susan to our seats at the time she said that to the audience. We stopped in our tracks as we had an emotional response. We exchanged a knowing and pained look. A shared stream of unspoken thoughts sped through our brains semi-consciously: "Ambrose belongs to God. We miss him. And yet, we are grateful that he belongs to God."

The belief that he belongs to God makes all the difference in my mental health and hope. Kimberly isn't the only one to teach me this lesson.

"Repay to Caesar what belongs to Caesar and to God what belongs to God" -Jesus Christ

"The Lord giveth and the Lord taketh away, blessed be the Lord" -Job

"Thank you, dear Jesus, for all you have given me, all you have taken away from me, and all you have left me" -St. Thomas More

"Let the children come to me, and do not prevent them; for the kingdom of heaven belongs to such as these." -Jesus Christ

"Offer it up!" -Dad

Each of these quotes reminds me that everything God provides us is ours to care for and offer back to God in service and love to Him. And this, as Kimberly indicated, includes our children.

With that mindset, I can choose to repay to God what belongs to God. I can refrain from being mad at God for taking away what I perceived as mine. I can refrain from asking God to return Ambrose to me. And instead, I can do as Dad often advised and "offer it up." I do so now and will do so again and again.

Dear Lord, I offer up all my pain, sorrow, guilt, and heartache to you. But most of all, I offer back Ambrose to you. I offer up all our joyful memories and all my love for my son to you. As you commanded, I return to you what is yours. I give you what you gave me. I give you my son, my love, and myself.

Thank you, dear Lord.
Amen

Questions for Reflection:

1. How does the realization that everything and everyone belongs to God impact your perspective on the loss of your child or loved one?
2. How does the concept of entrusting your child or loved one to God's care and providence resonate with you?

Thankful on Sept 13, 2021

(one year after the tragic day)

On the first anniversary of Ambrose's tragic day, Susan and I planned nothing special. I was originally trying to work. But after a few hours, it became obvious I was not going to be able to concentrate on work. So instead, Susan and I drafted this thank you note and created two gift bags of fruit and flowers. We dropped one off at the Alton Memorial ER and one at the Fosterburg Firehouse. We remain grateful for what they did on that day and what they do every day!

To the Fosterburg First Responders
and Alton Memorial ER staff,

One year ago today, 9/13/2020, you made a difference. Our three-year-old son, Ambrose Augustine Fleming, drowned in our sibling's backyard pool. This day was the most tragic and brutal day of our lives. However, you were there for us and for more people than you likely realize.

When your team arrived on the scene, we learned Ambrose had been in the pool too long. Getting a heartbeat or a breath proved impossible. Susan had been doing CPR and breaths via 911 and only was able to get water out of his belly, mouth, and nose. She never got a pulse or him to breathe. You arrived and did all you could, BUT you did not pronounce him DOA... which meant so much to us. As a father, I could see in your eyes that you cared and were committed to doing all you could for our sweet little boy. I saw pained expressions on your faces as you tried in the backyard. I saw sadness on your face when we arrived in the ER. I wanted to hug you, thank you, and comfort you. Yet, we all were in a stressed state, and I didn't know what to do. But you need to know that you did your job, you did it well, and you made a difference.

You see, the Alton Memorial ER staff continued to build on your first responder efforts, and Ambrose miraculously recovered a heartbeat. Before this starts to sound like the happy ending of a saved life, let me tell you that Ambrose didn't survive. Unfortunately, not every life can be saved. Yet, you work, doing what you can, regardless of the odds of success and the risk to your mental health. You experienced the tragedy with us and poured your hearts into your work, your patient, who was our precious son, and us. You showed kindness, compassion, and resolve. You got his heart beating, him breathing on a vent, and you airlifted Ambrose on to Children's Hospital.

There, Susan and I spent seven days with Ambrose in the ICU....waiting, hoping, and praying for a miracle. There, we made the difficult decision to donate Ambrose's organs. We knew it was the right thing to do. We wavered because we were clinging to hopes of a miracle or wanted to hold him in our arms until he breathed his last breath. We learned that was impossible to do if we were to donate his organs. Ultimately, we decided to donate his organs. His organs, the ones you kept alive, have saved the lives of at least three and helped more individuals. Your actions provided our child's kidneys to two St. Louis adult women about my wife's age. Because of your efforts, those two women have told us that they have been granted a second chance at life. Your decisions provided a liver to a 2-month-old baby boy in Illinois. Your commitment provided a beating heart to a 4-year-old sweet little girl, who is a year older than our Ambrose, and we also heard she is doing well. He also helped two regain their vision with his corneas. One was internationally, and the other was in the United States.

Our families have hung our heads in sadness and felt empty because of the loss of our Ambrose. However, when we look beyond ourselves and see us all as one body, we rejoice. We rejoice for the lives saved, and we thank you for saving those lives.

Enclosed is a small gesture of gratitude toward you for how you treated us and cared for our shared body and the impact you have had on our souls.

May God Bless You,
Gerard and Susan Fleming and Ambrose's siblings:
Jack, Isaac, Blaise, Geena, Tobias, Agnes, Vianney,
and a new baby to arrive around January 23

Questions for Reflection:

1. Who has been there for you during your difficulties? How can you thank them?
2. Who else might be struggling with the loss of your loved one? How can you lean on each other?

Answer to My Prayers

Scripture: Jeremiah 29:12–13

Today, while holding my one-year-old son, Vianney, he wanted to touch the wall hanging with bible quotes. Somehow, I knew he was going to point to the "answer your prayers" verse. I had looked at it yesterday and thought to myself with anger, "God didn't answer MY prayer." I know I've dealt with this before and accepted God's will, and found many ways God did answer my prayers. However, in my human weakness, I occasionally find myself reverting to being frustrated with God for not bringing Ambrose back to me. Even as I'm angry, I feel guilty for being so, as I know God has been so good. Yet, that's where I was and sometimes return.

After Vianney pointed to it, I stepped far away from it, but he reached for it again. I walked back up to it, and his finger once again landed on the "answer your prayers" section. I noticed it was on JER 29:12-13. "Then you will call upon me and come and pray to me, and I will hear you. You will seek me and find me; when you seek me with all your heart."

Hmm. Before this event, I asked God to improve my prayer life, increase faith, and grow closer to Christ. My prayer life was weak, and my prayers were infrequent and often stale.

Well, Ambrose's hospitalization and passing certainly had me seeking my dear Lord with all my heart. I prayed to Him and called upon Him like never before. I truly sought Him, found Him, and fully surrendered to Him.

Where else was I to go? I became closer to Him than at any other time in my life.

No, I didn't get what I was asking for at that moment. And I didn't get what I thought I needed. But God did answer my prayers.

I have kept a list of "fruits" that have grown out of this pile of manure. There are many - too many to list and far too many to describe. But the greatest is that I sought Christ and found Him.

Dear Lord, I call upon you today; I ask you to be in my life. Please help me to continue to call upon you. I need you. I love you.

Questions for Reflection:

1. Have you questioned why God didn't answer your prayers or why he allowed this to happen?
2. Have you experienced any fruits from this pile of manure?

On the
JOURNEY
God will...
save and protect you.
lead and direct your steps.
fight for you.
make a way for you.
answer your prayers.
GIVE WISDOM and UNDERSTANDING.
fill you with hope.
STRENGTHEN WITH POWER.
bless you with good things.
be faithful to the end.
Marriage
PRAYER
Lord help us to remember
when we first met and
the strong love
that grew between us.
Help us love in
practical ways
so that nothing
can divide us. May our
words be kind
and our thoughts gracious.
May we remain humble
enough to ask for
forgiveness
and wise enough
to freely give.

Sharing My Dirty Laundry

It's Saturday, the day I have scheduled on our family chore chart that I get to do my laundry. Yes, we have a schedule. We don't follow it well, but I try. My goal is to keep each child's laundry separate from one another and especially from mine. It prevents all kinds of sorting and figuring out whose clothes are whose and helps keep clothes in the correct rooms and closets. Anyone from a large family understands.

So, today was my laundry day, but the washing machine and dryer were running when I brought my clothes down. So, I left my basket in the queue. That sounds so organized. It just means I dropped it on the floor in front of the washing machine next to other baskets of unwashed clothes. After a couple of hours, I went to put my clothes in the wash and what did I find? They were already in the wash, and the cycle was complete. The only problem, whoever was kind enough to wash my clothes mixed them with a hodgepodge of towels, children's clothes, hot pads, and who knows what. Ugh. Managing my mindset, I tell myself that someone was helpful, I'm the one who left my clothes sitting in the queue, and that it's not that big of a deal. The good news is that the laundry is getting done.

I empty my clothes and the mix of other invading items into the dryer. As I reach the bottom of the washing machine basin, I see what looks to be brown leaves or rocks. I reach in and pick each one up in my hands. As I pull them out of the washing machine, my eyes can't discern what they are. So, I decided to leverage my other senses. I smell them. Ugh! It's poop!

Seriously, I'm holding poop in my hands. Not only that, but my clothes were also just washed in poop. I'm sure that helps provide that lovely fresh scent! Then, engaging in more mental stability techniques, I remind myself, this is just part of the deal. Just throw the poop in the trash, wash your hands, re-wash your clothes and move on to the next task. But before doing so, I've decided to capture both the insignificance and significance of the moment.

There are daily messy moments in this packed house of 7 kids, a Great Dane puppy, and two adults. That's an understatement. It's just plain messy.

But I feel immensely privileged and entirely blessed. The mess comes with the gift God has provided. The love exchanged between parent and child is impossible to describe and immeasurable. The cost to benefit ratio is entirely lopsided. I'm picturing a scale with a few pebbles of poop on one side and a mountain range of love on the other. I live for the smiling gratitude of Vianney, the thumb sucking eternal watchful eye of Ambrose, the sparkling eyes of sweet Agnes, the laughter and fun of Tobias, the hugs and motherly love of Geena, the boisterous bounce and dynamic dialogue of Blaise, the prayerful faith of Isaac, the loyal help of Jack, and the strength of Susan's love.

Yes, I occasionally find myself holding poop in my hands. But I am forever grateful to God for this beautiful family.

Questions for Reflection:

1. When your thoughts start to lead you astray, how do you manage your mindset?
2. What has helped you persevere through life's minor and major challenges?

The Veil Between Us

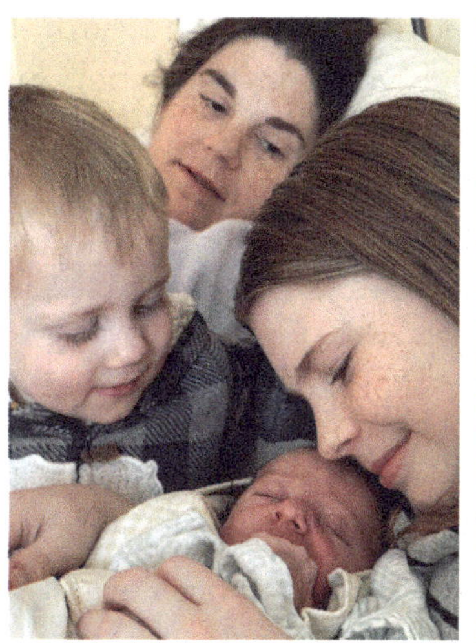

Good morning, Ambrose.

Today is two days after your little brother, Mateo, was born. It is a snowy day and Agnes asked me to get her snow boots out of the basement. That led me to the bins of shoes, and I saw your little sandals through the opaque bin. Oh, how the cloudy barrier of the bin between me and those sandals felt like a representation of your simultaneous presence and absence. It is like you are just on the other side of that foggy bin. I know you are there, but I can't see or touch you. After that, I had to go find your yellow hooded coat and hug it for a while. I was able to conjure up memories of holding you by doing so. It was as if I truly got to hug you and feel your head on my shoulder as the hood rested against my head. Sigh. I love and miss you.

Thank you for your intercession for the healthy birth of your little brother, for keeping Mom safe, and for being

there for his birth, even if from the other side of the veil between heaven and earth. I love you and miss you, my sweet beautiful son. Keep watching over your little brother and all of us.

Questions for Reflection:

1. Do you feel the presence of your loved one?
2. How do you keep the precious memories alive?
3. Do you trust in holding your loved one once again?

Good morning!

Vianney can't sleep, thank God.

At 4:00 a.m. Vianney came looking for me. He peeked his head in our door and smiled from the other side. I took him back to his bed. He laid down on the floor level bottom bunk of our new triple bunks. Wow, it just dawned on me that when we bought this bed we disposed of the bed that Ambrose used to sleep on. Not long after Ambrose passed, Vianney outgrew his crib and was moved into the place where Ambrose once slept. But the old double bunk where Blaise and Tobias slept was falling apart and I feared it may get dangerous. So we replaced the three beds with this triple bunk. I just can't believe I didn't get sentimental about disposing of not only Ambrose's bed but the setting of where he slept.

Anyway, back to 4:00 a.m., Vianney asked or told me to "Lay down. Lay down," as he tapped the bed in the space right next to his little body.

At 52 years old, I crawled and ducked onto the floor level bunk that held the mattress that Ambrose once slept on. Vianney made sure he was touching me as he laid there in bed. He was too tired to stay awake but also unable to fall asleep. As he laid up against me, with his little arm over my chest, I soaked in his love. I stroked his head, prayed for some intentions and some prayers of appreciation. Dear Lord, thank you for this beautiful boy. Thank you for his life. Look how his little fist rubs his eyes! Thank you that he is able to do that. See how he raised his eye lids to verify I was still present! Thank you God that his brain is fully functioning and his eyes can see me.

When Ambrose laid in that hospital bed, I stared at his precious little body and would have bounced off the walls as I celebrated any such movements. Oh to just see him rub his little nose! I think of Levi, a little boy who survived a drowning, and how every tiny act he initiates is celebrated by his parents. I take so much for granted but I'm learning to appreciate God's gifts more and more.

It would have been a legitimate option to not answer Vianney's request to lay down. I could have turned back to my own king-sized bed. But I didn't. Instead, I snuggled with my two year old, I blessed his head, I stroked his face, and I thanked God for this precious boy. And that has made all the difference.

Good morning!

Questions for Reflection:

1. What gifts has God given you that you have taken for granted?
2. How can you show someone you live with today that you love and appreciate them?

Happy Father's Day— An Opportunity to Love

This Father's Day morning, I woke up looking forward to heading downstairs to enjoy quiet time alone while the family slept. In this busy household and with my introverted personality, I appreciate early, peaceful Sunday morning time to read, pray, reflect, and journal.

I eagerly started to leave the bedroom when 4-month-old Mateo began crying. Susan asked, "Can you take him? I need to get some sleep?" Admittedly, my first thought was, "It's Father's Day, and I had plans to get some quiet time." Thankfully, this time, I remembered Father's Day was not about me getting the day off from being a husband and father. It's about honoring and respecting fathers' sacrificial love for their children.

In moments like this, I lean on the lesson Susan and

Ambrose taught me in September of 2020. The lesson Susan taught through her example was to love our children gratefully and sacrificially while we have the opportunity. When Ambrose was in the hospital, he expelled something vile. The nurse stated that it was the worst mess she'd seen come from a child or adult. Instead of getting some early morning rest and letting the nurse clean up Ambrose, Susan said, "This may be the last dirty diaper of his I ever get to change for him, so I am going to do it." Since then, when I face a dirty diaper (literally and figuratively), I say to myself, "Thank God, I get to do this." And I mean it.

So, I took inconsolable Mateo from Susan and let her sleep. I carried him downstairs, changed his diaper, and thanked God for this opportunity. Mateo smiled up at me, and God smiled down upon me. We spent some quiet time together and migrated to the front porch on this beautiful, peaceful Sunday morning. I sat on Ambrose's bench, prayed, and reflected on this Father's Day morning.

As I write this, I'm sitting on Ambrose's bench. The morning is still and quiet, with only the sound of birds chirping. A breeze, as gently as possible, brushes up against Ambrose's wind chime and plays a soft tone that says, "Hello Dad, I'm here with you, sharing in this peaceful moment. Happy Father's Day."

Questions for Reflection:

1. Are there fruitful lessons you have learned from this experience?
2. How has your loss helped you appreciate life, despite the challenges?
3. Has your loss helped you to view life from a new perspective?

A Father's Sacrificial Love

Scripture: Ezekiel 36:26

A new heart I will give you, and a new spirit I will put within you; and I will take out of your flesh the heart of stone and give you a heart of flesh.

I've been impacted by images of Christ's sacrificial, loving heart ever since my Dad passed away in 2016 when Mom gave me Dad's wallet. It contained 40 dollars and a Sacred Heart of Jesus badge.

The image of Christ's heart ablaze in love, wrapped in thorns, and topped with a cross, spoke to me. Christ loved us so much that he endured great suffering, including the crown of thorns, being pierced by a sword, and being nailed to a cross, so that we may have eternal life.

The fact that Dad carried it in his wallet inspired me. Dad visibly lived his faith, but he, first and foremost, inwardly lived it. The image was there every time he opened his wallet. Perhaps Dad kept it as a regular reminder of Christ's love and sacrifice for him. I do not know, but the image in his wallet conjures up thoughts of Dad's work, love, and sacrifices that he gave to countless others. Money, representing Dad's works, was one way Dad shared Christ's sacrificial love with others.

I began carrying Dad's Sacred Heart of Jesus badge in my wallet to remind myself to trust in Christ's sacrificial and merciful love, which grants us a pathway to eternal life. It reminds me that because of Christ's sacrificial love, I have hope of being with Dad once again. It reminds me to do as Dad often told me: offer up suffering to God and for others.

I kept that badge in my wallet for four years, not yet fully appreciating its meaning. But on a September day in 2020, I took the Sacred Heart of Jesus badge and placed it on my son Ambrose's chest as he lay in a PICU hospital bed. I prayed to Christ for the miracle of life.

I did not receive the miracle I prayed for, yet I did. Ambrose, my sweet little 3-year-old son, passed away. Yet, Ambrose's miracle was to save the lives of others by donating his organs. Among those he saved was a 4-year-old girl. Ambrose gave her his heart, enabling her to live. His heart! His most precious, beautiful, loving heart saved an equally precious little child of God.

There's something about it that reminds me of Christ's great sacrifice. I know it's not the same, but it is a tangible metaphor. Dad gave me his heart, his sacrificial love, and that Sacred Heart of Jesus badge. I gave the heart I received from Dad to Ambrose and placed it on his chest. Ambrose gave his heart to Callie, and the miracle of life continues.

God the Father loves us so much that he gave us his only Son. When I hear those words now, I feel the pain of losing my son and appreciate God the Father's gift. Then, His only Son loved us so much that He gave his life to save us. Jesus gave us his heart, his most Sacred Heart.

When I receive communion, I view it as a heart transplant. I think of Christ willingly donating his heart to me. He replaces my stony and broken heart with a living, fleshy, beating heart capable of loving so deeply that I may have eternal life.

I cannot fully fathom the love of the Heart of Christ – what he suffered and what we gained. It does not get any bigger than this. To give up one's life and suffer as much as He did! And for what?! Or better asked, for who? For me; for you; so that we may have eternal life.

Sacred Heart of Jesus, I place all my trust in you.

Questions for Reflection:

1. What does the image of the Sacred Heart mean to you?
2. What do you carry with you to remember your loved one or your faith?
3. How has your faith helped you heal?

In our Darkest Hours

I recently went camping in Eminence, MO. Late at night, when all the campfires were out and lights were off, I stood in the darkness, alone under a clear sky. As I looked up, I was in awe of the stars and how beautifully they shined!

In our darkest hours, that's when we can see the light best. All too often, as the light shines all around us, we take it for granted and don't even notice its existence. We may even forget it's there and all that it does for us. But in the darkness, the faintest light from millions of miles away shines beautifully and brightly upon us.

Dear Lord, lift up my head. Let me see the light of your love shining down on me. In times of comfort, let me not take your love for granted. Keep me from being so self-absorbed that I don't appreciate the love and kindness bestowed upon me. In times of darkness, remind me to lift my head and see the glory of God.

Questions for Reflection:

1. How have you seen God in your darkest hours?
2. What have you come to appreciate that you once took for granted?

Hope Heightened

Ambrose,

It's now two years since the day you drowned. I heard someone say on the radio today, "Grief is love realized." Her point is that we realize how deeply we love someone after they pass. Yes, and for me, "Grief is hope heightened." I love you; I miss you, and I have deep and faithful hope that I will see you again. Rest in Christ; rest in His love. I will hold you once again.

Love, Dad

Questions for Reflection:

1. What is hope?
2. How has your grief increased your faith and heightened your hope?
3. Do you pray for and/or to your loved one?

Letting Go of Your Things, Holding onto You

Susan and I took our daughter, Geena, to an American Heritage Girls retreat the other day. On the drive, Geena noticed old toys in the back of the car and asked what we were doing with them. I told her we were donating them. She got unusually quiet. I could sense something was up. I asked, "Is there something you don't want us to donate back there?"

She barely got out his name but softly said, "Ambrose." I was confused and said, "What?" She said, "The toy barn. It was his." My heart sank for her. I told her that I understood. I truly did. I also explained to Geena that we couldn't hold onto everything that was his. Besides, we have two of the same toys since Vianney received one for his birthday. Plus, we don't even know which one was Ambrose's and which was Vianney's. Geena corrected me, "I know which one was Ambrose's. See, this one doesn't have the sticker on the door and the...." She knew the subtle differences.

I told her we could keep the toy. After a short pause, she replied, "That's all right. I'm ready to let it go now."

The next day, I was alone in the car, running errands. Ambrose's toy barn rocked back and forth in my review mirror. It felt like a little hello from Ambrose, and I stopped at the gravesite on my way home.

Once there, I began my "round of prayers," walking around Ambrose's headstone. I first stopped at Ambrose's picture and gave his forehead the sign of the cross blessing like I used to do to him every night before he went to sleep. I asked him to intercede for his family, especially his siblings and a friend's son. Then, I focused on the lamb and thanked Jesus for his sacrifice. I moved to the Holy Family and prayed for my family. Then the marriage rings and for our marriage. I moved around the side to the Divine Mercy Jesus, where I asked Christ to shower his mercy upon us. Then, to the image of Susan with Mary and Ambrose and thanked Mary for her sorrowful compassion, and finally to the Pieta and asked our sorrowful mother to pray for us.

I returned to the car and saw that toy barn standing out among the pile of toys. I hesitated, thinking it was a little weird, but decided to place Ambrose's toy on his gravestone. And then I cried.

It's not so easy letting go. And I'm not going to. At least, not of you, Ambrose. I may (or may not) let go of your toys. But I will hold onto you forever. I love you.

Questions for Reflection:

1. Have you had difficulty letting go of items that once belonged to your loved one?
2. Do you visit the cemetery? Do you pray when you go there?
3. Where/How do you find peace?

AUGUSTINE
MING
OUR LADY OF SO
PRAY FOR U

In My Father's House

Scripture: Luke 2: 41-52

I imagine every parent has felt the anxiety of losing a child in a crowd, at a store, at the park, or elsewhere. I have a few memories of such stressful moments.

The first time I remember this happening was when my oldest son was about four, and we went to the St. Louis Balloon Race at Forest Park. We walked through a sitting crowd, watching the balloons light up at dusk. I must have let go of Jack's hand, taken a few steps forward, and then turned around. He was gone. I mean, just plain gone. I scoured the crowd in a panic. But everyone sitting on the ground was about the same height as little Jack, and he was nowhere to be seen. The next thing I know, he's standing right at my feet. I don't know how he got there or if he was ever really gone. But, oh, I felt such relief and joy when I found him right by my side.

In a recent Gospel reading, Luke 2: 41-51, Joseph and Mary temporarily lost their twelve-year-old, Jesus. Can you imagine the anxiety? They lost him for three days! When I lost Jack, it wasn't even three minutes. The three days of Jesus being "lost" seem to foreshadow Jesus being in the tomb for three days. In both situations, Jesus was apparently gone, but not truly gone, and certainly not permanently gone.

I lost another son. Ambrose passed away at three years old. He and his thumb-sucking smile are also apparently gone, but not truly gone, and certainly not permanently gone. Just as Joseph and Mary found Jesus in the Temple of his Father's house, I will one day find Ambrose in our same Father's house.

Dear Lord,

I miss Ambrose. There's an unexplainable emptiness due to the separation. It's like a gap between two magnetic poles meant to be together. I ask for your wisdom and strength in helping me use the energy from this gap to drive me toward union with you and him. Help me to find him in memory and prayer. May the memories of my sweet boy ignite a sense of gratitude for the gift you gave me. And may my prayers to my son bring me closer to you. I trust his life entirely with you and do not ask that you bring him back to me but rather that he brings me to you. May he draw me closer to the Holy Eucharist, where I will find him in union with you – giving up your bodies so we may have life.

Amen

Questions for Reflection:

1. Do you view your separation from your loved one as temporary?
2. When do you feel closest to your loved one who has passed away?
3. What does Jesus's resurrection mean to you?

One Body

Ambrose's death and gift of life have helped me better understand the concept of us all being part of one body: the body of Christ. When one part of this body suffers, we all suffer, and when one rejoices, we all rejoice. We rejoice and have sorrow simultaneously as we share this one body.

Agnes's profound stick drawing portrays the concept of one body and simultaneous emotions so beautifully. On one half of the piece of paper, she drew herself and explained that she was crying because her brother was dead. On the other half of the paper, she drew her dead brother in his casket and explained he was smiling because he was in heaven. Stepping back and looking at the entire image of them as one body illustrates the simultaneous emotions of joy and sorrow that my children felt as part of this one body. Agnes is sad but also happy for her brother's joy. Ambrose is eternally joyful yet has compassion for his sister's sorrow.

The same is true when we reflect on Ambrose's organ donation. Knowing that Ambrose provided life to others brings us great joy! And I know that while others celebrate the gift of life received, they also have deep, compassionate sorrow for our family.

We are more than connected. We are one body. The way my brothers and sisters in Christ came together to pray for us and love us 5 years ago, and since, has been healing. God's love and grace surrounded us and filled our hearts. Thank you for this extraordinary gift.

God is calling me to continuously accept the love of Christ that you have shared into my heart and I let it flow through and out of me so that I can share Christ's love back with you.

May you welcome Christ's love into your heart, let His love heal your soul, and continuously share His love with the rest of His body.

Amen

Questions for Reflection:

1. How have you experienced connectedness to others?
2. Have you had joy and sorrow simultaneously?

Want a hug, Daddy?

This morning's Father's Day became an emotional Ambrose memory morning. It started subtly when I noticed the wall-hanging rosary Agnes received for her first communion intertwined with Ambrose's wall-hanging rosary. When Agnes received it, she commented that it was like Ambrose's rosary. And in her love and desire to stay connected to her little brother, she twisted her rosary up with his.

A short moment later, I looked down and saw the photo album Susan had printed into a book of Ambrose's first year. I looked through the pages, remembered his big joyful smile, and found three pictures of Uncle Paul, whose funeral is coming up in two days, holding baby Ambrose. I told myself they were hugging once again, now in heaven.

Then I ate breakfast with Mateo. What a joy this little guy is to spend breakfast with. He smiles and stares into my eyes, his giant eyes emitting complete love. We played the game I've played with each of our little ones. We look away from one another, pretending to be focused on something else, and then quickly turn our heads back to face each other with a big laugh. It's a simple game but brings us joy. It has this subtle message that says, even when our eyes are not meeting, I'm thinking of you. I know you are there, and we will stare into each other's eyes again with pure joy and laughter.

Then Mateo started identifying himself and each of his siblings in the portraits hanging around our dining room table: "That's Jack?" and I'd reply, "Yes." He repeated it for each child but skipped over Ambrose's picture. My heart sank a little. Then, right outside the picture window, Ambrose's memorial wind chimes started playing their tune, letting me know he is still there even though we are not looking into each other's eyes.

That was it. I started to tear up. At this point, Mateo was playing with a truck on the floor but noticed me. He asked, "Are you okay, Daddy?" I nodded, but my tears told this little two-year-old boy the truth. He asked me, "Want a hug, Daddy?" as he climbed up onto my lap not awaiting an answer. Oh, that was the most amazing hug.

What a joy and blessing to be a father!

Questions for Reflection:

1. What holidays or dates lead you to reflect on your love for your child or loved one?
2. What games did you enjoy with your child or loved one?
3. How can we love others with the heart of a child?

Where am I?

Dear Lord,

In my darkest hours, I doubted your presence. I'm sorry. You were there with me. Of course, you were there! Thank you for revealing this to me. You are the good shepherd and friend who is there for me in my times of joy and in my times of suffering. I now realize that the question I need to ask myself in my times of suffering is not "Where is Jesus?" Rather, the question I need to ask myself is, "How can I be there for my Lord and my friend, Jesus, during His suffering?" Compassion means "to suffer together," and after some time, I recognized that you and Mary were there compassionately with me in my suffering.

And now, I realize that I should be a good friend and choose to be with you in your suffering. But how do I show compassion for you, my dear Lord? In my fear and grief, let me not flee but follow you. As you sweat blood in agony in the Garden, let me be by your side praying, together asking God the Father to let our suffering pass, yet accepting God's will be done. As you carry your heavy cross, let me walk by your side carrying my much lighter cross. As you ask the Father to forgive those who inflicted unimaginable suffering upon you, help me to forgive.

And as you conquered death and rose again in your transformed and glorified body, let me allow myself to trust in your mercy and your promise. Help me also transform by accepting your loving heart, lifting up my head, and sharing your love with others. As you retained your wounds in your resurrected, glorified body, let me radiate your love while my wounds remain as signs of your victory over death.

Dear Lord, I want to be your good friend and remain with you in your joy and suffering. Thank you for allowing me to unite my sufferings with yours. Thank you for giving my pain and sorrow the ultimate purpose. Through all of this, you have increased my faith, heightened my hope, and inspired me to love. Like Thomas, now that I have joined you, and entered into your wounds, I see you and I know you. Thank you, my Good Shepherd, my dear friend, my Lord, and my God. Thank you.

Amen

Questions for Reflection:

1. Have you been there for others in their time of suffering and sorrow?
2. Have you tried to unite your suffering with Jesus' suffering?
3. How has your sorrow brought you closer to Christ?

Embracing Christ

A couple days after Mateo was born (3 years ago), Agnes wanted a pair of snow boots. The journey to the basement brought me to Ambrose's little brown sandals. The sandals my three-year-old little boy, Ambrose, wore throughout the summer of 2020 and finally to Grandma's house on Sept 13, 2020. Seeing those sandals hidden behind a foggy bin was analogous to Ambrose being on the other side of the veil between heaven and earth. I looked beyond the shoes over to find Ambrose's little yellow coat hanging up among other winter garments. I grabbed that coat and hugged the memory of Ambrose and I imagined his head filled the hood and rested on my shoulder.

Very early this morning, Mateo woke me up. As I heard him by my side, my first thought was to tell him to go back to bed. I had to check that thought as I've learned to appreciate even the inconveniences of raising a child. Instead of sending him away, I stroked his little face and asked him what he wanted. He had wet his bed and asked for help getting showered and clean clothes on.

After getting him cleaned up, we then enjoyed a silly and intimate breakfast together. I love praying before meals with him. Mateo prays with me so well and corrects me when I adjust the words to the prayer. This morning, I said, "Bless us O Lord and these thy gifts that Mateo and I are about to receive...." Mateo stopped me as he said, "that's not right!" with a big grin on his face. I ended the prayer with a "and thank you for our noses and our ears" as I pressed his nose and gently touched his ears. Again, he corrected me, "that's not right." And then, when I finish the prayer, he emphatically and in his deepest scratchy voice, shouts out, "Now let's eat!". It makes me smile every time.

I moved to the couch with my cup of coffee, preparing for some quiet morning prayer time. I have some heavy things on my heart that I am anxious to bring to the Lord in prayer – a friend with colon cancer, another with infertility, another with a son who was back on track but seems to have taken a detour, and so many other intentions. As I began to pray, Mateo came up to me and asked if he could go outside and play. I told him that he needed to get his coat on, because it's cold outside. He returned wearing Ambrose's yellow coat and asked me to button it for him. The scene put me in a time warp. It was as if I was looking at Ambrose and Mateo at the same time. Instead of buttoning his coat, I snatched Mateo up into my arms and gave him an extra tight and prolonged hug. At first, he just received the hug in a state of confusion with his arms down. But then, he wrapped those little arms tightly around me, squeezed with all his might, and then rested his little hooded head on my shoulder. And then, he adjusted his head positioning (something the empty yellow coat didn't ever do), and I thanked God for Mateo and his health.

Give those loved ones of yours an extra tight and prolonged hug today. And thank God for the gift!

Dear Lord,

Thank you for the gifts of Mateo, all my children, Susan, my family, and friends. Help me to embrace the love that surrounds me—the love that is right in front of me. Help me to recognize that your love flows through them. Let me experience Ambrose's love, my parents' love, and your divine love as one united stream, flowing through the precious souls I am graced to be with today. Dear Lord, help me to embrace your Sacred Heart.

Amen.

Questions for Reflection

1. How is Christ's love present in your life?
2. Do you see the gift of life right in front of you?
3. Do you trust that your life is a gift?

Closing Remarks

When people ask me how to journey through grief, I often share the simple yet profound wisdom a young priest once offered me. One week after the funeral, as Susan and I stepped out of Sunday Mass, Fr. Alexander Nord greeted us and asked gently, "Do you mind if I give you unsolicited advice?" His words were brief but enduring: "Lean on each other."

The following week, he found us again after Mass and asked, "Can I give you more unsolicited advice?" This time, he said, "It's okay to be happy." That second offering was surprisingly just as healing as the first.

Lean on Each Other

Susan and I have leaned on each other through our grief. We tend to grieve in different ways and waves, often in silence—but the grace of sharing sorrow and love has been immeasurable. Some of our most healing moments have come when we cried together, or simply held one another in quiet understanding. In leaning on each other, we have held each other up.

Leaning on one another also means leaning on Mary and Jesus. In prayer, I've imagined myself beside Mary at the foot of the Cross, physically leaning on her. She holds me up. I've also returned in prayer to the tragic day when

I collapsed in agony, grasping at the grass and crying out. At that moment, I was transported to the Garden of Gethsemane. There, beside me, was Jesus—on His hands and knees, grasping the earth. He turned to me, and in that gaze we shared a profound empathy. We were both suffering, yet each was more concerned for the other.

I also lean on the communion of saints—those I trust are in union with Christ in heaven: Mom, Dad, Ambrose, and others I've loved. I speak to them, ask for their intercession, and seek their guidance. This practice gives me perspective. They are not dead and gone; they are alive in Christ, radiant with joy. I pray for them too, not knowing the state of their souls, but trusting in God's mercy and wisdom.

Leaning on one another includes receiving the kindness and support of those who have offered a listening ear or lifted us in prayer. Through their love, I have tangibly encountered Christ. Friends, acquaintances, even strangers have reached out with compassion. They have prayed, listened, and shared their own journeys. From their acts of love, I've learned two things: the importance of being a vessel of Christ's love to others and the grace of allowing others to be that vessel for me.

I'm leaning on you, my brothers and sisters in Christ, who also mourn someone deeply loved. Thank you for walking this path with me. We are not alone. As we listen to one another and bear witness to each other's grief, we comfort one another and grow in faith.

It's Okay to Be Happy

When Fr. Nord shared this bit of advice, it caught me off guard. I honestly wasn't quite sure how to take it. The funeral was just two weeks ago and he's talking about being happy! Part of me thought, Well, there goes his advice-giving batting average.

As I sat with his words, another part of me recognized their truth. There's a photo I keep of Susan that I call her Pietà moment. We were in the hospital, and she was cradling Ambrose's lifeless body. The agony on her face is unmistakable—grief etched into every line, suffering that reached the depths of her soul.

But what the photo doesn't show is something that amazed and inspired me. About ten minutes after I took that picture, Susan was still holding Ambrose in her lap. My sisters were present, and they began talking. Someone said something that made us laugh—and Susan laughed too. That image, of my wife smiling through her sorrow, gave me hope. It was a glimpse of joy in the midst of devastation.

And there is reason for joy. The Resurrection is not merely coming—it has already happened. We live in its light. We can trust in God's goodness, even when the path is steep and the pain is raw.

On the day of Ambrose's drowning, Susan said something that has stayed with me: "No matter what happens, it's going to be okay." She was right. We know how the story ends. It's going to be okay. And yes—it's okay to be happy.

Closing with Prayer

Dear Lord,

Thank you for this community of grievers who have joined together in reflection and prayer. Bless them, their families and their loved ones. Help them to receive your love into their hearts. Transplant their broken, grieving hearts with your fleshy loving heart. Give them a heart of gratitude and joy. Be by their side bringing them comfort as you shower down your endless love and mercy upon them. Give them the courage to receive your love, to lift up their heads and pour your love upon others. Dear Lord, I ask that you heighten their hope, deepen their faith, and expand their love.

Amen

Made in the USA
Coppell, TX
21 January 2026

69143893R00046